JAN 2013

What are
seeds?

D1716407

by Molly Aloian

 Crabtree Publishing Company

www.crabtreebooks.com

Plants Close-Up

Author
Molly Aloian

Publishing plan research and development
Sean Charlebois, Reagan Miller
Crabtree Publishing Company

Editors
Reagan Miller, Kathy Middleton

Proofreader
Kathy Middleton

Notes to adults
Reagan Miller

Photo research
Allison Napier, Ken Wright, Crystal Sikkens

Design
Ken Wright

**Production coordinator and
Prepress technician**
Ken Wright

Print coordinator
Katherine Berti

Photographs
Thinkstock: title page, page 7 (left), 10, 12, 13, 16, 22, 23
Shutterstock: pages 11, 14, 19, 21
Other images by Shutterstock and Thinkstock

Library and Archives Canada Cataloguing in Publication

Aloian, Molly
    What are seeds? / Molly Aloian.

(Plants close-up)
Includes index.
Issued also in electronic formats.
ISBN 978-0-7787-4221-0 (bound).--ISBN 978-0-7787-4226-5 (pbk.)

    1. Seeds--Juvenile literature. 2. Plant anatomy--Juvenile
literature. I. Title. II. Series: Plants close-up

QK661.A46 2012   j581.4'67   C2012-900412-X

Library of Congress Cataloging-in-Publication Data

Aloian, Molly.
    What are seeds? / Molly Aloian.
        p. cm. -- (Plants close-up)
    Includes index.
    ISBN 978-0-7787-4221-0 (reinforced library binding : alk. paper) --
    ISBN 978-0-7787-4226-5 (pbk. : alk. paper) -- ISBN 978-1-4271-7906-7
    (electronic pdf) -- ISBN 978-1-4271-8021-6 (electronic html)
    1. Seeds--Juvenile literature. I. Title.

    QK661.A46 2012
    581.4'67--dc23
                                            2012001128

Crabtree Publishing Company

www.crabtreebooks.com   1-800-387-7650

Printed in the U.S.A./102012/SN20120907

Published in Canada
Crabtree Publishing
616 Welland Ave.
St. Catharines, Ontario
L2M 5V6

Published in the United States
Crabtree Publishing
PMB 59051
350 Fifth Avenue, 59th Floor
New York, New York 10118

Published in the United Kingdom
Crabtree Publishing
Maritime House
Basin Road North, Hove
BN41 1WR

Published in Australia
Crabtree Publishing
3 Charles Street
Coburg North
VIC 3058

Contents

Plants make seeds

Seeds are living things. Seeds are made by plants. Plants are living things, too.

New plants grow from seeds. Seeds can be many sizes, colors, and shapes. A new plant will be the same kind of plant its seed came from.

Plant parts

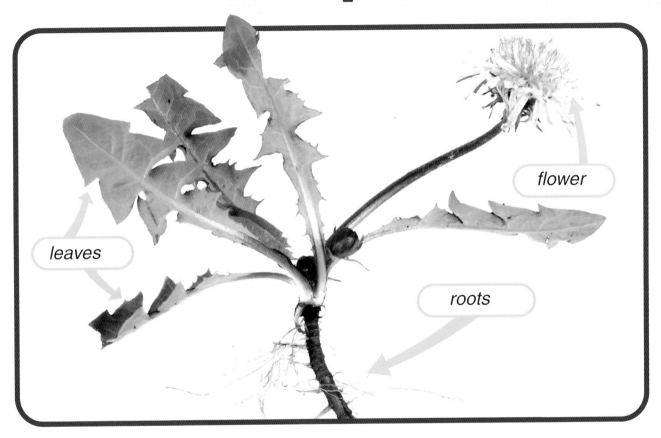

leaves

flower

roots

All plants have roots, stems, and leaves. Some plants have flowers and some have fruit. Seeds are contained in the plant's flowers or fruit.

Some seeds are large. An avocado fruit has one big seed inside. Other seeds are tiny. A poppy flower has a lot of tiny seeds inside.

poppy seeds

avocado seed

New plants

Seeds grow into new plants. Seeds need water, air, nutrients, and sunlight to grow into new plants.

seeds

Some flowers contain many seeds.

Others contain only a few seeds.

This sunflower contains many seeds.

What is a seed?

seed food

A seed contains all the food that the new plant will need to begin to grow. This food is called **seed food**.

seed coat

Each seed has a **seed coat** to protect the new plant inside the seed. A seed coat is an outer covering. Some are smooth. Some are rough.

Hiding inside

seedpod

The seeds of some plants grow together in a case called a **seedpod**. The pod splits open to release the seeds when they are ready to grow.

The seeds of evergreen trees are found in cones. Evergreen trees have needles for leaves.

A place to grow

When the seeds of some plants are ready to grow, they drop off the plant and land in the soil underneath.

Some seeds have parts, or **structures**, that help them travel farther away. The wind carries these seeds and scatters them in new growing places.

Floating on water

Plants that live in water have small seeds that float to new growing spots.

The seeds sink and begin growing at the bottom of a lake, pond, or other waterway. The stems of the water lily flowers in this picture reach all the way to the bottom of this lake.

Spreading seeds

Some seeds are spread by animals.

For example, a seed eaten by a squirrel is carried inside the squirrel's body to a new place.

The seed is released by the squirrel in its droppings, and the seed begins to grow.

A seed sprouts

seedling

shoot

seed case

When a seed starts to grow in soil, we say it **sprouts**. First, the seed case breaks open. A tiny root grows into the soil to get water and nutrients.

Then, a shoot grows upward to get sunlight and air. The shoot grows into a young plant called a seedling. When it is fully grown, the plant will make its own seeds.

Seeds called grains

Some seeds, called **grains**, are food for us to eat.

wheat

The seeds of wheat and oats are used to make cereal, bread, and other foods we eat. These plants are called cereal grasses.

Words to know

grains 22

seed coat 11

seed food 10

seedpod 12

sprouts 20

structures 15

Notes for adults and activities

• **Seed sorting:**
Instructions to adults: Cut a variety of fruits and vegetables open to reveal the seeds. Pass them around for children to explore with their senses. Discuss how seeds are different in size and shape. Encourage children to think of different ways that they could sort the seeds.

• **What is inside a seed?**
Instructions to adults: Soak bean seeds in water overnight. Ask children to remove the seed coat. Ask them why seeds have a seed coat. (To protect the new plant inside the seed.) Open the two halves of the seed and find the tiny leaves, stem, and root of the young plant. Show children how to use a magnifying glass to observe and identify the parts of a seed. Discuss the functions of each seed part. Have children draw a picture of their seed and label the parts.

Learn more

Books

Plants are living things (Introducing Living Things) by Bobbie Kalman. Crabtree Publishing Company (2007)

A Bean s Life (Crabtree Connections) by Angela Royston. Crabtree Publishing Company (2011)

Websites

The Great Plant Escape: Children team up with Detective LePlant to identify plant parts and functions and explore how a plant grows.
http://urbanext.illinois.edu/gpe/index.cfm

Michigan 4-H Children's Garden Tour: This interactive site takes visitors on a virtual garden tour. Children learn about different kinds of plants, play educational games, and answer questions.
http://4hgarden.msu.edu/kidstour/tour.html